France

For Kids

People, Places and Cultures
Children Explore The World Books

BABY PROFESSOR
EDUCATION KIDS

Speedy Publishing LLC
40 E. Main St. #1156
Newark, DE 19711
www.speedypublishing.com

Let's learn some interesting facts about France!

France is officially known as the French Republic.

The name France comes from the Latin word Francia, which means 'country of the Franks'.

The official language is French.

**French is the
second most
studied language
in the world
after English.**

France is the most visited country in the world, with over 80 million visitors every year.

The famous Eiffel Tower in Paris was built as the entrance point for the 1889 World Fair. It is one of the most visited monuments in the world.

France was the second country to host the modern Olympic Games in 1900 in Paris.

The most famous road bicycle race in the world, the Tour de France zig zags through the French landscape.

France's highest mountains are the French Alps and Jura Mountains, bordering Italy and Switzerland, and the Pyrénées, along the frontier with Spain.

More than
350 kinds
of cheese
are made
in France.

Tomme des
Bauges
12E50 Le Kg

Tomme de
VACHE
14E50 Kg

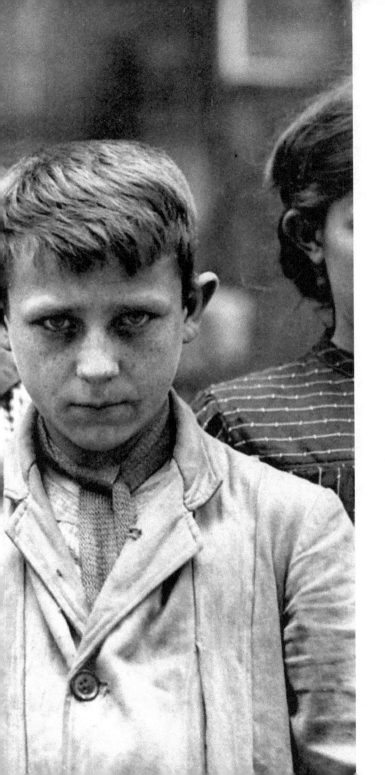

France has laws about naming children. Until 1993, all names had to be chosen from an official list. Today, public prosecutors can still reject a child's name.

Soccer, bicycling and tennis are favorite sports in France. In some areas, pelote, a traditional handball game, is popular.

The school day typically runs from 8:00 a.m. to 4:00 p.m., with a two-hour lunch break. Schools close Wednesday and Sunday, and have a half-day on Saturday.

France still retains 15 territories overseas – this includes Martinique, Guadeloupe, French Guiana, Réunion and Mayotte.

Bastille Day is celebrated on July 14th in France. The day is celebrates the storming of The Bastille and the beginning of the French Revolution.

The countryside of France is very scenic. There are many orchards, farms, and vineyards among France's peaceful villages.

Cannes is a world
famous resort
in France that
is known for the
International
Film Festival that
takes place there
every May.

France has a lot to offer and you should visit the country soon and explore!